THE GREAT BOOK OF CA!

AN EDUCATIONAL CAMBODIA TRAVEL FACTS WITH PICTURE BOOK FOR KIDS ABOUT HISTORY, DESTINATION PLACES, ANIMALS, AND MANY MORE

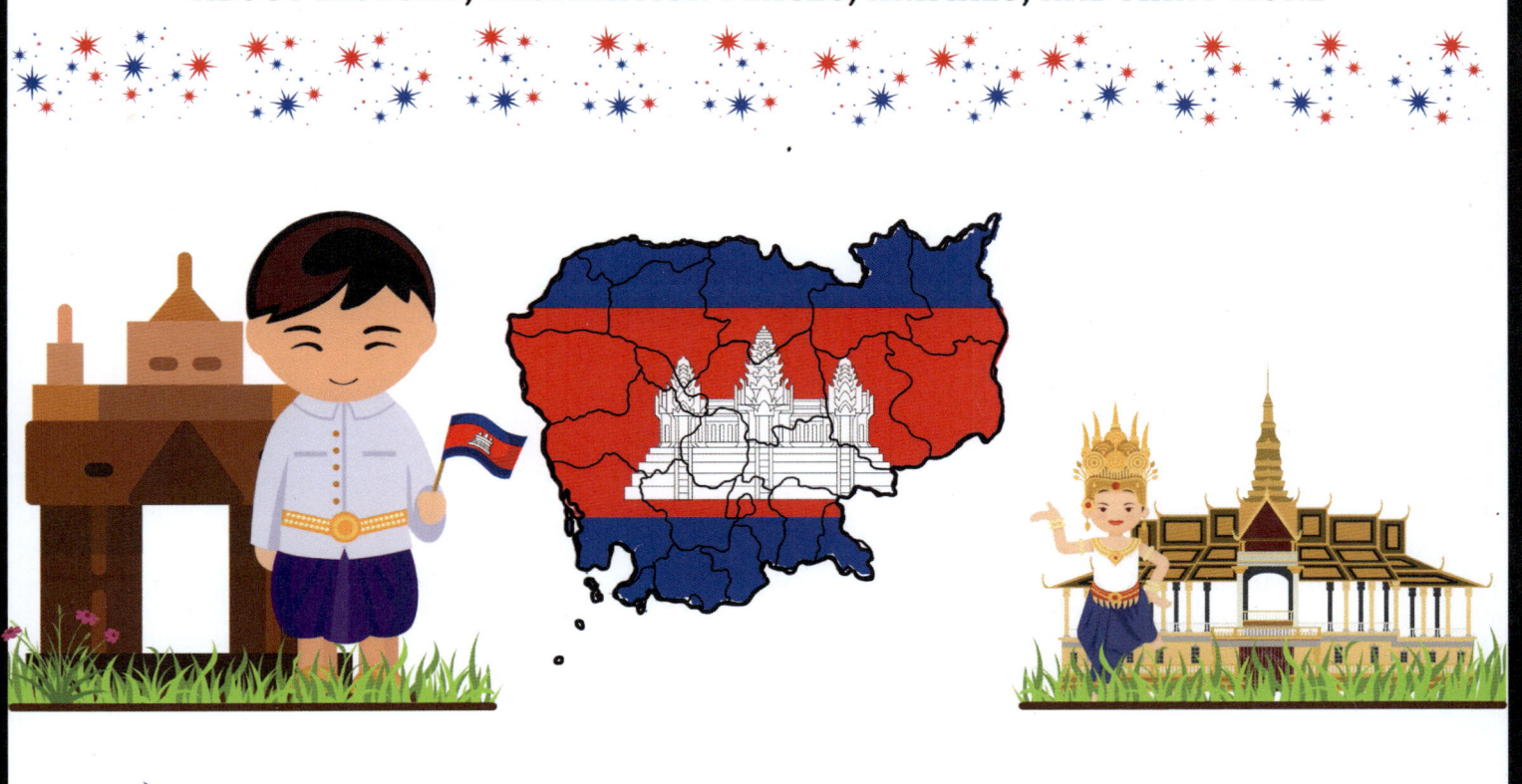

Copyright @2023 James K. Mahi

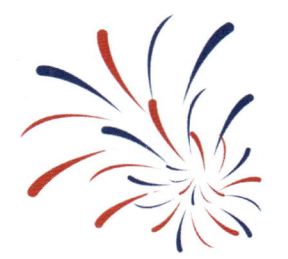

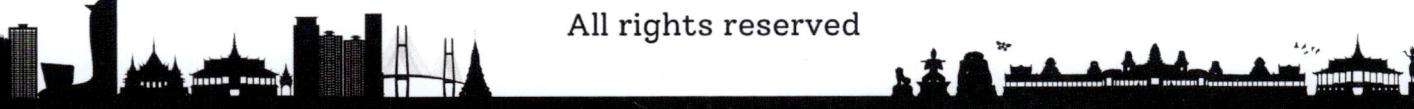

All rights reserved

Cambodia is **located in Southeast Asia,** bordered by Thailand to the northwest, Laos to the northeast, Vietnam to the east, and the Gulf of Thailand to the southwest.

Which continent does Cambodia belong to?

Cambodia is located in Southeast Asia.

How many countries does Cambodia border?

Cambodia shares borders with three countries: Thailand, Laos, and Vietnam.

How big is Cambodia?

Cambodia ranks 88th in the world by land area, with a landmass of 176,520 square kilometers (68,155 square miles).

What percentage of the world's land does Cambodia occupy?

Cambodia occupies about 0.24% of the world's land area.

What percentage of Cambodia is covered by rainforests?

Approximately 60% of Cambodia is covered by rainforests.

Which city is the largest in Cambodia?

Phnom Penh is the largest city in Cambodia.

How many provinces does Cambodia have?

Cambodia is divided into 25 provinces.

What is the population of Cambodia?

Cambodia's population was around 16 million.

What is the population of Cambodia?

Cambodia's population density is relatively moderate compared to some countries. However, population distribution varies across the regions.

What are the people of Cambodia called?

The people of Cambodia are called Cambodians.

What is Cambodia's literacy rate?

Cambodia's literacy rate was around 83.2%.

What is the national animal of Cambodia?

The Kouprey, a wild ox, is the national animal of Cambodia.

What is the national bird of Cambodia?

The Giant Ibis is the national bird of Cambodia.

What is the national sport of Cambodia?

The national sport of Cambodia is Bokator, an ancient Khmer martial art.

What is the national tree of Cambodia?
The national tree of Cambodia is the Sugar Palm, also known as Tnaot in Khmer and scientifically named Borassus flabellifer.

What is the official name of Cambodia?

The official name of Cambodia is the Kingdom of Cambodia.

How many time zones are there in Cambodia?
Cambodia operates on a single time zone, which is Indochina Time (ICT), UTC+7.

What is Cambodia's nickname?
Cambodia is often referred to as the "Kingdom of Wonder."

Who ruled Cambodia first?

The ancient Khmer Empire, with its capital in Angkor, was among the first to rule Cambodia. The empire existed from the 9th to the 15th century.

Which months are the coldest in Cambodia?
Cambodia generally experiences warm temperatures throughout the year, and there isn't a distinct cold season.

Which months are the hottest in Cambodia?
The hottest months in Cambodia are typically April and May.

Why do tourists visit Cambodia?
Tourists visit Cambodia to explore its rich history, ancient temples (such as Angkor Wat), vibrant culture, and natural landscapes. The country offers a unique and diverse travel experience.

How many visitors visit Cambodia every year?

Cambodia attracted several million visitors annually.

The capital and largest city of Cambodia is **Phnom Penh.**

The official language of Cambodia is **Khmer**.

The currency used in Cambodia is **the Cambodian Riel (KHR)**.

Cambodia is known for its rich history, including the ancient Khmer Empire, which built the famous Angkor Wat temple complex.

Angkor Wat is the largest religious monument in the world and is a UNESCO World Heritage site.

The Khmer Empire, which existed from the 9th to the 15th centuries, was one of the most powerful empires in Southeast Asia.

Cambodia has a monarchy, and the current king is Norodom Sihamoni.

The country has a tropical climate, with a **rainy season from May to October** **and a dry season from November to April.**

Cambodia has a diverse range of wildlife, including **elephants, tigers, and various species of monkeys.**

The Irrawaddy dolphin, a unique freshwater dolphin species, can be found in the Mekong River in Cambodia.

The official religion of Cambodia is Theravada Buddhism, and many temples and pagodas can be found throughout the country.

The traditional Cambodian dance, known as Apsara dance, is a classical dance form that originated in the royal courts.

Cambodia celebrates its New Year, known as Choul Chnam Thmey, in April. It is a time of festivities, family gatherings, and cleansing rituals.

NOVEMBER 9 INDEPENDENCE DAY

Cambodia gained independence from French colonial rule on November 9, 1953.

The famous Temple of Bayon, located in the Angkor Thom complex, is known for its many giant stone faces.

Cambodia has a tragic history related to the Khmer Rouge regime, which ruled the country from 1975 to 1979. The regime led to the death and suffering of millions of Cambodians.

The Killing Fields, located near Phnom Penh, are a somber reminder of the atrocities committed during the Khmer Rouge era.

Cambodia has a unique culinary tradition, **with dishes like Amok (a coconut milk-based curry)** and Lok Lak (stir-fried beef) being popular.

The Royal Palace in Phnom Penh is a stunning example of Khmer architecture and serves as the residence of the king.

The Cardamom Mountains in Cambodia are home to diverse ecosystems and endangered species.

Cambodia is home to **the largest population of the endangered Indochinese tiger.**

The ancient city of Angkor was the capital of the Khmer Empire and is now a major archaeological site.

The country is known for its **silk weaving,** producing intricate patterns and designs.

The famous Silver Pagoda in Phnom Penh is known for its floor made of over 5,000 silver tiles.

Cambodia is famous for its floating villages, where houses are built on stilts to cope with the seasonal changes in water levels.

The famous Silver Pagoda in Phnom Penh is known for its floor made of over 5,000 silver tiles.

The Elephant Terrace in Angkor Thom features intricate carvings of elephants and other mythical creatures.

Cambodia has a diverse range of traditional festivals, **including the Water Festival, Boat Racing Festival, and Pchum Ben (Ancestors' Day).**

The Preah Vihear Temple, located on the border with Thailand, is another UNESCO World Heritage site.

The official name of Cambodia is the Kingdom of Cambodia.

Cambodia has a vibrant traditional music scene, and instruments like the Khmer harp and tro sau are commonly used.

The Tonle Sap River changes its flow direction twice a year, creating the Tonle Sap Great Lake.

Cambodia's flag was adopted in 1948, and the depiction of Angkor Wat symbolizes the country's cultural heritage.

Cambodia's national motto is "Nation, Religion, King."

The ancient city of Angkor was rediscovered in the 19th century by French explorer Henri Mouhot.

Cambodia is home to the endangered giant ibis, one of the rarest bird species in the world.

The Khmer Rouge's reign of terror led to the destruction of many cultural artifacts and historical sites.

The Ta Prohm temple, known for being overgrown by massive tree roots, gained fame through its appearance in the movie "Lara Croft: Tomb Raider."

The Koh Ker temple complex, located in the northern jungles, was briefly the capital of the Khmer Empire.

The Angkor National Museum in Siem Reap showcases artifacts from the Angkor temples.

The Sampeah is a traditional Cambodian greeting, where the palms are pressed together in a prayer-like gesture.

ESSENTIAL FACTS FOR TRAVELERS VISITING CAMBODIA:

1. **Visa Requirements:** Most visitors to Cambodia need a visa. You can obtain one on arrival at the airport or border crossing, or apply for an e-visa online before your trip.
2. **Currency:** The official currency is the Cambodian Riel (KHR), but US dollars are widely accepted. It's advisable to carry small denominations in both currencies.
3. **Local Customs:** Cambodian culture emphasizes modesty and respect. When visiting temples, dress modestly, covering your shoulders and knees. Remove your shoes before entering someone's home or a religious site.
4. **Language:** Khmer is the official language, but English is commonly spoken in tourist areas. Learning a few basic Khmer phrases can enhance your experience.
5. **Weather Considerations:** Cambodia has a tropical climate with a distinct wet and dry season. Be prepared for high temperatures and humidity, especially during the hot season from March to June.
6. **Health Precautions:** Check if vaccinations are required before traveling. Malaria is present in some areas, so consult with a healthcare professional about preventive measures.
7. **Transportation:** Tuk-tuks are a popular and affordable mode of transportation in cities. Use reputable transportation services, and negotiate prices before getting in.
8. **Bargaining Culture:** Bargaining is common in markets and with street vendors. Polite negotiation is expected, and it's part of the local shopping experience.
9. **Safety:** While Cambodia is generally safe for tourists, it's essential to stay vigilant, especially in crowded areas. Take standard precautions to safeguard your belongings.
10. **Electricity:** The standard voltage is 230V, and the power outlets are of type A, C, and G. Bring suitable adapters if needed.

Printed in Great Britain
by Amazon